THE GOSPEL ACCORDING TO

JOHN

with Introduction by

Henry Wansbrough OSB

All booklets are published thanks to the
generous support of the members of the
Catholic Truth Society

CATHOLIC TRUTH SOCIETY
PUBLISHERS TO THE HOLY SEE

Contents

The Jerusalem Bible translation

The Jerusalem Bible was first published in 1966. It was produced by a team of distinguished English scholars (including J.R.R. Tolkien), working under Alexander Jones. It made available for English readers the findings of the French *Bible de Jérusalem* published a decade earlier by the famous French biblical school in Jerusalem, the first Catholic Bible edition to incorporate all the advances of modern biblical study. The Jerusalem Bible was the first translation of the whole Bible into modern English, and as such has maintained its status as authorised for use in the liturgy.

❧ INTRODUCTION ❧

John and the Synoptic Gospels

The fourth gospel is a challenge to the reader. It is very different from the other, synoptic, gospels. The outline pattern is different: the synoptics show Jesus making a single, week-long visit to Jerusalem at the end of his ministry, but John shows him making four separate visits to Jerusalem. In the synoptics Jesus' opponents are described as Sadducees, Pharisees and scribes; in John Sadducees and scribes are not mentioned, and the opponents are described overwhelmingly as 'the Jews'. The synoptic gospels are built from short, independent incidents, sayings and parables; John contains no parables, and many fewer incidents. But these much longer incidents, described in detail, with extended dialogue, often develop into reflective and meditative discourses by Jesus or the evangelist. Most significant of all, in the synoptics Jesus is bent on establishing the Sovereignty or Kingdom of God, while in John the Kingdom of God is mentioned only once, and Jesus principally reveals himself and his relationship to the Father. Paradoxically, the portrait of Jesus is at once the most human and the most transcendent of the gospel portraits, so that Augustine wrote, 'John, as though scorning to tread upon earth, rose by his very first words not only above the earth, above the atmosphere, above the

3

heavens, but even above the whole army of angels and all the array of invisible powers'.

In a previous age scholars considered that John was the least reliable historically. More recently it has become apparent that many of the historical details in John are superior to those of the synoptics. Where John and the synoptics both have a saying, the form given in John is often more primitive. The author's familiarity with the city of Jerusalem and the surrounding country is considerably more detailed. Of course it remains true that, especially in the longer discourses, Jesus often speaks in a style which is quite unlike that of the pithy sayings reported by the synoptics, and markedly similar to John's own meditative style.

The structure of the gospel is also a puzzle: several sections of the gospel seem detachable or misplaced. The poetic and theological prologue (1:1-18) is of a quite different stamp to the rest of the gospel. The final chapter seems to be an additional epilogue, making a new start after the concluding verses, 20:20-21, reiterated in 21:25. Chapter 6 on the Bread of Life may have been inserted to illustrate the statement about Moses in 5:45. The Raising of Lazarus (chapter 11) seems to have been added after the conclusion to Jesus' public ministry in 10:40-42. There seem to be three versions of the Discourse after the Last Supper, which partially overlap (chapters 14, 15-16 and 17). Nevertheless, there are traits of style running

4

throughout the gospel which show that the final version is the work of one mind. Throughout, there is the technique of the puzzled question ('How can this man give us his flesh to eat?' 6:52) to advance the dialogue, ambiguity (is 'living water' in 4:10 merely fresh water or the Water of Life? When Jesus is to be 'lifted up', 12:32, is this lifted up on the Cross or to heaven?) and above all, irony. (The Pharisees berate the man born blind, when all the time it is they who cannot see 9:13-34.) Caiaphas proposes that one man should die to save the people (11:49), failing to grasp what he is really saying. The Roman soldiers mock Jesus as king of the Jews (19:3) which the reader knows to be really the case. Similarly, Pilate publicly declares the same, refusing the plea of the Jewish leaders that Jesus merely claimed this title (19:21-22).

The Author of the Gospel

The identity of this author remains mysterious. Tradition associates this gospel with John the Apostle, son of Zebedee. The two sons of Zebedee feature strongly in the synoptic gospels, but are never mentioned in John. Traditionally this has been explained as self-denying reticence by John, who merely gives himself the code-name 'the Beloved Disciple'. It has, however, been asked why this Disciple occurs only in the Jerusalem stories, how he was 'known to the High Priest' (18:16), if he was a Galilean fisherman. It has even been suggested that the disciple whom Jesus loved, who is at the origin of the tradition of the gospel, is Lazarus (see 11:3,11,36). Others have suggested that the Beloved Disciple is a symbolic figure standing for any disciple whom Jesus loves, close to Jesus at the Eucharist (13:23), sharing the Passion with Jesus and with his mother forming the first Christian community (19:26-27), believing in the Resurrection (20:8), and custodian for ever of the Christian message (21:22-24).

The Messiah of Judaism - and more

An opposition - or bipolarity - is at the heart of the gospel; 'He came to his own and his own received him not' (1:10). They preferred darkness to light, blindness to sight, falsehood to truth, death to life. They searched the scriptures but refused to come to Jesus to whom the scriptures testify (5:39). This blindness is greater in that throughout the gospel Jesus is seen to sum up in his person the values and festivals of Judaism. At a first series of encounters the disciples acknowledge him as Rabbi, Messiah, Son of God and King of Israel (1:38-49). At Cana he turns water, always the symbol of the life-giving Law, into the wine of the messianic wedding-feast, and the disciples saw his glory (2:1-11). In the Temple the Jews cannot accept that his body, risen after three days, will replace the Temple (2:13-22). At the Pool of Bethzatha he makes the Sabbath his own by working the cure of the sick man (5:1-18). At the Passover he shows that he, not the manna which Moses gave to their fathers in the desert, is the true bread from heaven (6:4-33). At the feast of Tabernacles, the festival of water, he claims that his Spirit is the water which quenches all thirst (7:1-38). At the winter Festival of Light he claims to be the light of the world (8:12). Finally he dies on the Cross at the moment the lambs were being slaughtered for Passover (1:29; 19:36).

All the time the theme of judgement hovers in the background. The language of the lawcourts abounds: truth, falsehood, witness, condemn. The Father has given all judgement to the Son, but the Son judges no one. The followers of Jesus and his opponents judge themselves by their favourable or adverse reaction to Jesus, until the dreadful scene before Pilate. With typical Johannine irony the Jewish leaders think they are condemning Jesus, when in fact they are condemning themselves before Jesus crowned as king and judge, when they reject the true King of Israel by crying out, 'We have no king but Caesar' (19:15).

John insists that Jesus is human. In no other gospel do we see Jesus tired and hungry (4:6-7), weeping at the death of his friend (11:36). Yet his knowledge is beyond that of any human being. He sees Nathanael under the fig-tree (1:48, compare 2:25; 6:6; 7:14-31). He speaks of his own pre-existence (6:64; 8:58). He knows all about his future Passion (13:1), maintains his sovereign control even when he is dying on the Cross, and even in death has the power to take up his life again (10:17-18). This is because the purpose of his coming is to reveal the Father, for he and the Father are one: 'whoever has seen me has seen the Father (14:9-10). Rather than by any static definition, this is made clearest by the dynamic equivalence of the Son with the Father; 'the Son can do only what he sees the Father doing, and whatever the Father does he does too' (5:19). The powers to give life and to judge belong exclusively to God, but it is precisely these powers that the Father has given to the Son (5:21-30). This goes well beyond any acceptable explanation of Jesus in function of the terminology of Judaism, the extremity of confrontation being reached when Jesus takes for himself the divine name itself, 'Before Abraham was, I AM' (8:58,28). In the Temple the Jews react by preparing to stone him for blasphemy, while the arresting-party in the Garden respond to the same claim by falling to the ground in involuntary worship (18:6). Paradoxically, the climax of the revelation of the oneness of Father and Son comes at the glorification of the Son in the Hour of his Passion, their perfect unity and love being shown in the obedience of the Son (17:1-23).

The Spirit of Jesus

In the course of the gospel there is repeated mention of the Spirit who will lead the disciples into full knowledge of the truth; during the ministry of Jesus this Spirit had not yet come (2:22; 4:23; 7:39). In the final discourses after the

Last Supper Jesus speaks of the Paraclete or 'Advocate', whom the Father will send at his request (14:26), or whom he will himself send, issuing from the Father (15:26). This Spirit will come to the help of the disciples and lead them into all truth (14:16-17), making Christ present when he has parted from them. At his death on the Cross, with typical Johannine ambiguity, Jesus 'gave up his spirit' (19:30), and at the first appearance of the Risen Christ in the upper room he breathes this Holy Spirit on the disciples (20:22). It is clear that this Spirit even now makes Christ present in the world through worship (4:23), through the authority granted to his disciples and in the sacraments of baptism (3:5) and eucharist (6:63). This awareness, already during the ministry of Jesus, of the Spirit who will make the life of Jesus present to the community of his followers, constitutes a major difference from the synoptic gospels, where the expectation is all on the return of Christ at the end of time.

Reading John

Many authors have likened John to an eagle circling high in the skies. John meditates loftily on the elevated truths about Christ from different angles. This gospel especially must be read reflectively and slowly in order to appreciate the many different levels of meaning which are often only hinted at. The prologue particularly is a wonderful treasury of the revelation imparted by the body of the gospel, and a summary of the tensions involved in the confrontations between the Word made flesh, his own people who did not accept him and those to whom he gave power to become children of God. It is rewarding to return to it again and again in the course of a reading of the gospel.

The Gospel According to
❧ John ❧

Prologue

1 *¹In the beginning was the Word:
and the Word was with God
and the Word was God.
²He was with God in the beginning.
³Through him all things came to be,
not one thing had its being but through him.
⁴All that came to be had life in him
and that life was the light of men,
⁵a light that shines in the dark,
a light that darkness could not overpower.*[a]

*⁶A man came, sent by God.
His name was John.
⁷He came as a witness,
as a witness to speak for the light,
so that everyone might believe through him.
⁸He was not the light,
only a witness to speak for the light.*

*⁹The Word was the true light
that enlightens all men;*

---

[a] Or 'grasp', in the sense of 'enclose' or 'understand'.

and he was coming into the world.
[10]He was in the world
that had its being through him,
and the world did not know him.
[11]He came to his own domain
and his own people did not accept him.
[12]But to all who did accept him
he gave power to become children of God,
to all who believe in the name of him
[13]who was born not out of human stock
or urge of the flesh
or will of man
but of God himself.
[14]The Word was made flesh,
he lived among us[b],
and we saw his glory,
the glory that is his as the only Son of the Father,
full of grace and truth.

[15]John appears as his witness. He proclaims:
'This is the one of whom I said:
He who comes after me
ranks before me
because he existed before me'.

[1 b.] 'pitched his tent among us'.

*[16]Indeed, from his fulness we have, all of us, received -
yes, grace in return for grace,
[17]since, though the Law was given through Moses,
grace and truth have come through Jesus Christ.
[18]No one has ever seen God;
it is the only Son, who is nearest to the Father's heart,
who has made him known.*

I. THE FIRST PASSOVER

A. The Opening Week

The witness of John

[19]This is how John appeared as a witness. When the Jews[c] sent priests and Levites from Jerusalem to ask him, 'Who are you?' [20]he not only declared, but he declared quite openly, 'I am not the Christ'. [21]'Well then,' they asked 'are you Elijah?'[d] 'I am not' he said. 'Are you the Prophet?'[e] He answered, 'No'. [22]So they said to him, 'Who are you? We must take back an answer to those who sent us. What have you to say about yourself?' [23]So John said, 'I am, as Isaiah prophesied:

*a voice that cries in the wilderness:
Make a straight way for the Lord'.*[f]

---

[c] In Jn this usually indicates the Jewish religious authorities who were hostile to Jesus; but occasionally the Jews as a whole.
[d] whose return was expected, Ml 3:23-24.
[e] The Prophet greater than Moses who was expected as Messiah, on an interpretation of Dt 18:15.
[f] Is 40:3

²⁴Now these men had been sent by the Pharisees, ²⁵and they put this further question to him, 'Why are you baptising if you are not the Christ, and not Elijah, and not the prophet?' ²⁶John replied, 'I baptise with water; but there stands among you - unknown to you - ²⁷the one who is coming after me; and I am not fit to undo his sandal-strap'. ²⁸This happened at Bethany, on the far side of the Jordan, where John was baptising.

²⁹The next day, seeing Jesus coming towards him, John said, 'Look, there is the lamb of God that takes away the sin of the world. ³⁰This is the one I spoke of when I said: A man is coming after me who ranks before me because he existed before me. ³¹I did not know him myself, and yet it was to reveal him to Israel that I came baptising with water.' ³²John also declared, 'I saw the Spirit coming down on him from heaven like a dove and resting on him. ³³I did not know him myself, but he who sent me to baptise with water had said to me, "The man on whom you see the Spirit come down and rest is the one who is going to baptise with the Holy Spirit". ³⁴Yes, I have seen and I am the witness that he is the Chosen One of God.'

The first disciples

³⁵On the following day as John stood there again with two of his disciples, ³⁶Jesus passed, and John stared hard at him and said, 'Look, there is the lamb of God'. ³⁷Hearing this, the two disciples followed Jesus. ³⁸Jesus turned round, saw them following and said, 'What do you

want?' They answered, 'Rabbi,' - which means Teacher - 'where do you live?' [39]'Come and see' he replied; so they went and saw where he lived, and stayed with him the rest of that day. It was about the tenth hour[g].

[40]One of these two who became followers of Jesus after hearing what John had said was Andrew, the brother of Simon Peter. [41]Early next morning, Andrew met his brother and said to him, 'We have found the Messiah' - which means the Christ - [42]and he took Simon to Jesus. Jesus looked hard at him and said, 'You are Simon son of John; you are to be called Cephas' - meaning Rock.

[43]The next day, after Jesus had decided to leave for Galilee, he met Philip and said, 'Follow me'. [44]Philip came from the same town, Bethsaida, as Andrew and Peter. [45]Philip found Nathanael[h] and said to him, 'We have found the one Moses wrote about in the Law, the one about whom the prophets wrote: he is Jesus son of Joseph, from Nazareth'. [46]'From Nazareth?' said Nathanael 'Can anything good come from that place?' 'Come and see' replied Philip. [47]When Jesus saw Nathanael coming he said of him, 'There is an Israelite who deserves the name, incapable of deceit'. [48]'How do you know me?' said Nathanael. 'Before Philip came to call you,' said Jesus, 'I saw you under the fig tree.' [49]Nathanael answered, 'Rabbi, you are the Son of God,

---

[g] 4 p.m.

[h] Probably the Bartholomew of the other gospels.

15

you are the King of Israel'. ⁵⁰Jesus replied, 'You believe that just because I said: I saw you under the fig tree. You will see greater things than that.' ⁵¹And then he added 'I tell you most solemnly, you will see heaven laid open and, above the Son of Man, the angels of God ascending and descending'.

The wedding at Cana

2 ¹Three days later there was a wedding at Cana in Galilee. The mother of Jesus was there, ²and Jesus and his disciples had also been invited. ³When they ran out of wine, since the wine provided for the wedding was all finished, the mother of Jesus said to him, 'They have no wine'. ⁴Jesus said 'Woman, why turn to me? My hour has not come yet.' ⁵His mother said to the servants, 'Do whatever he tells you'ᵃ. ⁶There were six stone water jars standing there, meant for the ablutions that are customary among the Jews: each could hold twenty or thirty gallons. ⁷Jesus said to the servants, 'Fill the jars with water', and they filled them to the brim. ⁸'Draw some out now' he told them 'and take it to the steward.' ⁹They did this; the steward tasted the water, and it had turned into wine. Having no idea where it came from - only the servants who had drawn the water knew - the steward called the bridegroom ¹⁰and said; 'People generally serve the best wine first, and keep the cheaper sort till the guests have had

---

²ᵃ Gn 41:55

plenty to drink; but you have kept the best wine till now'.

[11]This was the first of the signs given by Jesus: it was given at Cana in Galilee. He let his glory be seen, and his disciples believed in him. [12]After this he went down to Capernaum with his mother and the brothers, but they stayed there only a few days.

B. The Passover

The cleansing of the Temple

[13]Just before the Jewish Passover Jesus went up to Jerusalem, [14]and in the Temple he found people selling cattle and sheep and pigeons, and the money changers sitting at their counters there. [15]Making a whip out of some cord, he drove them all out of the Temple, cattle and sheep as well, scattered the money changers' coins, knocked their tables over [16]and said to the pigeon-sellers, 'Take all this out of here and stop turning my Father's house into a market'. [17]Then his disciples remembered the words of scripture: *Zeal for your house will devour me.*[b] [18]The Jews intervened and said, 'What sign can you show us to justify what you have done?' [19]Jesus answered, 'Destroy this sanctuary, and in three days I will raise it up'. [20]The Jews replied, 'It has taken forty-six years to build this sanctuary[c]: are you going to raise it up in three days?' [21]But

---

[b.] Ps 69:9
[c.] Reconstruction work on the Temple began in 19 B.C. This is therefore the Passover of 28 A.D.

he was speaking of the sanctuary that was his body, ²²and when Jesus rose from the dead, his disciples remembered that he had said this, and they believed the scripture and the words he had said.

²³During his stay in Jerusalem for the Passover many believed in his name when they saw the signs that he gave, ²⁴but Jesus knew them all and did not trust himself to them; ²⁵he never needed evidence about any man; he could tell what a man had in him.

C. The Mystery of the Spirit
Revealed to a Master in Israel

The conversation with Nicodemus

3 ¹There was one of the Pharisees called Nicodemus, a leading Jew, ²who came to Jesus by night and said, 'Rabbi, we know that you are a teacher who comes from God; for no one could perform the signs that you do unless God were with him'. ³Jesus answered:

'I tell you most solemnly,

unless a man is born from above,

he cannot see the kingdom of God'.

⁴Nicodemus said, 'How can a grown man be born? Can he go back into his mother's womb and be born again?' ⁵Jesus replied:

'I tell you most solemnly,

unless a man is born through water and the Spirit,

he cannot enter the kingdom of God:

18

⁶what is born of the flesh is flesh;

what is born of the Spirit is spirit.

⁷Do not be surprised when I say:

You must be born from above.

⁸The wind blows wherever it pleases;

you hear its sound,

but you cannot tell where it comes from or where it is going.

That is how it is with all who are born of the Spirit.'

⁹'How can that be possible?' asked Nicodemus. ¹⁰'You, a teacher in Israel, and you do not know these things!' replied Jesus.

¹¹'I tell you most solemnly,

we speak only about what we know

and witness only to what we have seen

and yet you people reject our evidence.

¹²If you do not believe me

when I speak about things in this world,

how are you going to believe me

when I speak to you about heavenly things?

¹³No one has gone up to heaven

except the one who came down from heaven,

the Son of Man who is in heaven;

and the Son of Man must be lifted up

¹⁴as Moses lifted up the serpent in the desert,

¹⁵so that everyone who believes may have eternal life in him.

¹⁶Yes, God loved the world so much

that he gave his only Son,

so that everyone who believes in him may not be lost
but may have eternal life.
[17]For God sent his Son into the world
not to condemn the world,
but so that through him the world might be saved.
[18]No one who believes in him will be condemned;
but whoever refuses to believe is condemned already,
because he has refused to believe
in the name of God's only Son.
[19]On these grounds is sentence pronounced:
that though the light has come into the world
men have shown they prefer
darkness to the light
because their deeds were evil.
[20]And indeed, everybody who does wrong
hates the light and avoids it,
for fear his actions should be exposed;
[21]but the man who lives by the truth
comes out into the light,
so that it may be plainly seen that what he does
is done in God.'

II. JOURNEYS IN SAMARIA AND GALILEE

John bears witness for the last time

[22]After this, Jesus went with his disciples into the Judaean
countryside and stayed with them there and baptised. [23]At the

same time John was baptising at Aenon[a] near Salim, where there was plenty of water, and people were going there to be baptised. [24]This was before John had been put in prison.

[25]Now some of John's disciples had opened a discussion with a Jew about purification, [26]so they went to John and said, 'Rabbi, the man who was with you on the far side of the Jordan, the man to whom you bore witness, is baptising now; and everyone is going to him'. [27]John replied:

'A man can lay claim
only to what is given him from heaven.
[28]'You yourselves can bear me out: I said: I myself am not the Christ; I am the one who has been sent in front of him.
[29]'The bride is only for the bridegroom;
and yet the bridegroom's friend,
who stands there and listens,
is glad when he hears the bridegroom's voice.
This same joy I feel, and now it is complete.
[30]He must grow greater,
I must grow smaller.
[31]He who comes from above
is above all others;
he who is born of the earth
is earthly himself and speaks in an earthly way.
He who comes from heaven
[32]bears witness to the things he has seen and heard,

---

[a] A tradition locates Aenon ('Springs') in the Jordan valley, 7m. from Scythopolis.

even if his testimony is not accepted;
[33]though all who do accept his testimony
are attesting the truthfulness of God,
[34]since he whom God has sent
speaks God's own words:
God gives him the Spirit without reserve.
[35]The Father loves the Son
and has entrusted everything to him.
[36]Anyone who believes in the Son has eternal life,
but anyone who refuses to believe in the Son
     will never see life:
the anger of God stays on him.'

The saviour of the world revealed to the Samaritans

4 [1]When Jesus heard that the Pharisees had found out that he was making and baptising more disciples than John - [2]though in fact it was his disciples who baptised, not Jesus himself - [3]he left Judaea and went back to Galilee. [4]This meant that he had to cross Samaria.

[5]On the way he came to the Samaritan town called Sychar[a], near the land that Jacob gave to his son Joseph. [6]Jacob's well is there and Jesus, tired by the journey, sat straight down by the well. It was about the sixth hour[b]. [7]When a Samaritan woman came to draw water, Jesus said to her, 'Give me a drink'. [8]His disciples had gone

---

[a] Either Shechem (Aramaic: Sichara), or Askar at the foot of Mt Ebal.
'Joseph's Well' is not mentioned in Gn.
[b] Noon.

into the town to buy food. ⁹The Samaritan woman said to him, 'What? You are a Jew and you ask me, a Samaritan, for a drink?' - Jews, in fact, do not associate with Samaritans. ¹⁰Jesus replied:

'If you only knew what God is offering
and who it is that is saying to you:
Give me a drink,
you would have been the one to ask,
and he would have given you living water'.

¹¹'You have no bucket, sir,' she answered 'and the well is deep: how could you get this living water? ¹²Are you a greater man than our father Jacob who gave us this well and drank from it himself with his sons and his cattle?' ¹³Jesus replied:

'Whoever drinks this water
will get thirsty again;
¹⁴but anyone who drinks the water that I shall give
will never be thirsty again:
the water that I shall give
will turn into a spring inside him, welling up to eternal life'.

¹⁵'Sir,' said the woman 'give me some of that water, so that I may never get thirsty and never have to come here again to draw water.' ¹⁶'Go and call your husband' said Jesus to her 'and come back here.' ¹⁷The woman answered, 'I have no husband'. He said to her, 'You are right to say, "I have no husband"; ¹⁸for although you have had five, the one you have now is not your husband. You spoke the truth there.' ¹⁹'I see you are a prophet, sir' said

the woman. [20]'Our fathers worshiped on this mountain[c], while you say that Jerusalem is the place where one ought to worship.' [21]Jesus said:

'Believe me, woman, the hour is coming
when you will worship the Father
neither on this mountain nor in Jerusalem.
[22]You worship what you do not know;
we worship what we do know:
for salvation comes from the Jews.
[23]But the hour will come - in fact it is here already -
when true worshippers will worship the Father
    in spirit and truth:
that is the kind of worshipper
the Father wants.
[24]God is spirit,
and those who worship
must worship in spirit and truth.'

[25]The woman said to him, 'I know that Messiah - that is, Christ - is coming; and when he comes he will tell us everything'. [26]'I who am speaking to you,' said Jesus 'I am he.'

[27]At this point his disciples returned, and were surprised to find him speaking to a woman, though none of them asked, 'What do you want from her?' or, 'Why are you talking to her?' [28]The woman put down her water

---

[4c.] Gerizim, the mountain on which the Samaritans built a rival to the Jerusalem Temple; it was destroyed by Hyrcanus, 129 B.C.

jar and hurried back to the town to tell the people.
²⁹'Come and see a man who has told me everything I ever
did; I wonder if he is the Christ?' ³⁰This brought people
out of the town and they started walking towards him.

³¹Meanwhile, the disciples were urging him, 'Rabbi, do
have something to eat; ³²but he said, 'I have food to eat that
you do not know about'. ³³So the disciples asked one another,
'Has someone been bringing him food?' ³⁴But Jesus said:

'My food
is to do the will of the one who sent me,
and to complete his work.
³⁵Have you not got a saying:
Four months and then the harvest?
Well, I tell you:
Look around you, look at the fields;
already they are white, ready for harvest!
Already ³⁶the reaper is being paid his wages,
already he is bringing in the grain for eternal life,
and thus sower and reaper rejoice together.
³⁷For here the proverb holds good:
one sows, another reaps;
³⁸I sent you to reap
a harvest you had not worked for.
Others worked for it;
and you have come into the rewards of their trouble.'

³⁹Many Samaritans of that town had believed in him on
the strength of the woman's testimony when she said, 'He

told me all I have ever done', ⁴⁰so, when the Samaritans came up to him, they begged him to stay with them. He stayed for two days, and ⁴¹when he spoke to them many more came to believe; ⁴²and they said to the woman, 'Now we no longer believe because of what you told us; we have heard him ourselves and we know that he really is the saviour of the world'.

The cure of the nobleman's son

⁴³When the two days were over Jesus left for Galilee. ⁴⁴He himself had declared that there is no respect for a prophet in his own country, ⁴⁵but on his arrival the Galileans received him well, having seen all that he had done at Jerusalem during the festival which they too had attended.

⁴⁶He went again to Cana in Galilee, where he had changed the water into wine. Now there was a court official there whose son was ill at Capernaum ⁴⁷and, hearing that Jesus had arrived in Galilee from Judaea, he went and asked him to come and cure his son as he was at the point of death. ⁴⁸Jesus said, 'So you will not believe unless you see signs and portents!' ⁴⁹'Sir,' answered the official 'come down before my child dies.' ⁵⁰'Go home,' said Jesus 'your son will live.' The man believed what Jesus had said and started on his way; ⁵¹and while he was still on the journey back his servants met him with the news that his boy was alive. ⁵²He asked them when the boy had begun to recover. 'The fever left him yesterday' they said 'at the seventh hour.' ⁵³The father realised that

this was exactly the time when Jesus had said, 'Your son will live'; and he and all his household believed.

[54]This was the second sign given by Jesus, on his return from Judaea to Galilee.

III. THE SECOND FEAST AT JERUSALEM

The cure of a sick man at the Pool of Bethzatha

5 [1]Some time after this there was a Jewish festival, and Jesus went up to Jerusalem. [2]Now at the Sheep Pool in Jerusalem there is a building, called Bethzatha in Hebrew, consisting of five porticos; [3]and under these were crowds of sick people - blind, lame, paralysed - waiting for the water to move; [4]for at intervals the angel of the Lord came down into the pool, and the water was disturbed, and the first person to enter the water after this disturbance was cured of any ailment he suffered from. [5]One man there had an illness which had lasted thirty-eight years, [6]and when Jesus saw him lying there and knew he had been in this condition for a long time, he said, 'Do you want to be well again?' [7]'Sir,' replied the sick man 'I have no one to put me into the pool when the water is disturbed; and while I am still on the way, someone else gets there before me.' [8]Jesus said, 'Get up, pick up your sleeping-mat and walk'. [9]The man was cured at once, and he picked up his mat and walked away.

Now that day happened to be the sabbath, [10]so the Jews said to the man who had been cured, 'It is the sabbath; you are not allowed to carry your sleeping-mat'. ¹¹He replied, 'But the man who cured me told me, "Pick up your mat and walk"'. ¹²They asked, 'Who is the man who said to you, "Pick up your mat and walk"?' ¹³The man had no idea who it was, since Jesus had disappeared into the crowd that filled the place. ¹⁴After a while Jesus met him in the Temple and said, 'Now you are well again, be sure not to sin any more, or something worse may happen to you'. ¹⁵The man went back and told the Jews that it was Jesus who had cured him. ¹⁶It was because he did things like this on the sabbath that the Jews began to persecute Jesus. ¹⁷His answer to them was, 'My Father goes on working, and so do I'. ¹⁸But that only made the Jews even more intent on killing him, because, not content with breaking the sabbath, he spoke of God as his own Father, and so made himself God's equal. ¹⁹To this accusation Jesus replied:

'I tell you most solemnly,
the Son can do nothing by himself;
he can do only what he sees the Father doing:
and whatever the Father does the Son does too.
²⁰For the Father loves the Son
and shows him everything he does himself,
and he will show him even greater things than these,
works that will astonish you.
²¹Thus, as the Father raises the dead and gives them life,
so the Son gives life to anyone he chooses;
²²for the Father judges no one;

he has entrusted all judgement to the Son,
[23]so that all may honour the Son
as they honour the Father.
Whoever refuses honour to the Son
refuses honour to the Father who sent him.
[24]I tell you most solemnly,
whoever listens to my words,
and believes in the one who sent me,
has eternal life;
without being brought to judgement
he has passed from death to life.
[25]I tell you most solemnly,
the hour will come - in fact it is here already -
when the dead will hear the voice of the Son of God,
and all who hear it will live.
[26]For the Father, who is the source of life,
has made the Son the source of life;
[27]and, because he is the Son of Man,
has appointed him supreme judge.
[28]Do not be surprised at this,
for the hour is coming
when the dead will leave their graves
at the sound of his voice:
[29]those who did good
will rise again to life;
and those who did evil, to condemnation.
[30]I can do nothing by myself;

I can only judge as I am told to judge,
and my judging is just,
because my aim is to do not my own will,
but the will of him who sent me.

[31]'Were I to testify on my own behalf,
my testimony would not be valid;
[32]but there is another witness who can speak on my behalf,
and I know that his testimony is valid.
[33]You sent messengers to John,
and he gave his testimony to the truth:
[34]not that I depend on human testimony;
no, it is for your salvation that I speak of this.
[35]John was a lamp alight and shining
and for a time you were content to enjoy
        the light that he gave.
[36]But my testimony is greater than John's:
the works my Father has given me to carry out,
these same works of mine
testify that the Father has sent me.
[37]Besides, the Father who sent me
bears witness to me himself.
You have never heard his voice,
you have never seen his shape,
[38]and his word finds no home in you
because you do not believe
in the one he has sent.

[39]'You study the scriptures,
believing that in them you have eternal life;
now these same scriptures testify to me,
[40]and yet you refuse to come to me for life!
[41]As for human approval, this means nothing to me.
[42]Besides, I know you too well:
you have no love of God in you.
[43]I have come in the name of my Father
and you refuse to accept me;
if someone else comes in his own name
you will accept him.

[44]How can you believe,
since you look to one another for approval
and are not concerned
with the approval that comes from the one God?
[45]Do not imagine that I am going to accuse you
         before the Father:
you place your hopes on Moses,
and Moses will be your accuser.
[46]If you really believed him
you would believe me too,
since it was I that he was writing about;
[47]but if you refuse to believe what he wrote,
how can you believe what I say?'

IV. ANOTHER PASSOVER, THE BREAD OF LIFE

The miracle of the loaves

6 [1]Some time after this, Jesus went off to the other side of the Sea of Galilee - or of Tiberias - [2]and a large crowd followed him, impressed by the signs he gave by curing the sick. [3]Jesus climbed the hillside, and sat down there with his disciples. [4]It was shortly before the Jewish feast of Passover.

[5]Looking up, Jesus saw the crowds approaching and said to Philip, 'Where can we buy some bread for these people to eat?' [6]He only said this to test Philip; he himself knew exactly what he was going to do. [7]Philip answered, 'Two hundred denarii would only buy enough to give them a small piece each'. [8]One of his disciples, Andrew, Simon Peter's brother, said, [9]'There is a small boy here with five barley loaves and two fish; but what is that between so many?' [10]Jesus said to them, 'Make the people sit down'. There was plenty of grass there, and as many as five thousand men sat down. [11]Then Jesus took the loaves, gave thanks, and gave them out to all who were sitting ready; he then did the same with the fish, giving out as much as was wanted. [12]When they had eaten enough he said to the disciples, 'Pick up the pieces left over, so that nothing gets wasted'. [13]So they picked them up, and filled twelve hampers with scraps left over from the meal of five barley loaves. [14]The people, seeing this sign that he had given, said, 'This really is the prophet

who is to come into the world'. [15]Jesus, who could see they were about to come and take him by force and make him king, escaped back to the hills by himself.

Jesus walks on the waters

[16]That evening the disciples went down to the shore of the lake and [17]got into a boat to make for Capernaum on the other side of the lake. It was getting dark by now and Jesus had still not rejoined them. [18]The wind was strong, and the sea was getting rough. [19]They had rowed three or four miles when they saw Jesus walking on the lake and coming towards the boat. This frightened them, [20]but he said, 'It is I. Do not be afraid.' [21]They were for taking him into the boat, but in no time it reached the shore at the place they were making for.

The discourse in the synagogue at Capernaum

[22]Next day, the crowd that had stayed on the other side saw that only one boat had been there, and that Jesus had not got into the boat with his disciples, but that the disciples had set off by themselves. [23]Other boats, however, had put in from Tiberias, near the place where the bread had been eaten. [24]When the people saw that neither Jesus nor his disciples were there, they got into those boats and crossed to Capernaum to look for Jesus. [25]When they found him on the other side, they said to him, 'Rabbi, when did you come here?' [26]Jesus answered:

'I tell you most solemnly,

you are not looking for me

because you have seen the signs

but because you had all the bread you wanted to eat.

[27]Do not work for food that cannot last,

but work for food that endures to eternal life,

the kind of food the Son of Man is offering you,

for on him the Father, God himself, has set his seal.'

[28]Then they said to him, 'What must we do if we are to do the works that God wants?' [29]Jesus gave them this answer, 'This is working for God: you must believe in the one he has sent'. [30]So they said, 'What Sign will you give to show us that we should believe in you? What work will you do? [31]Our fathers had manna to eat in the desert; as scripture says: *He gave them bread from heaven to eat*'[a].

[32]Jesus answered:

'I tell you most solemnly,

it was not Moses who gave you bread from heaven,

it is my Father who gives you the bread from heaven,

the true bread;

[33]for the bread of God

is that which comes down from heaven

and gives life to the world'.

[34]'Sir,' they said 'give us that bread always.' [35]Jesus answered:

'I am the bread of life.

He who comes to me will never be hungry;

he who believes in me will never thirst.

---

[a] Ex 16:4f

³⁶But, as I have told you,
you can see me and still you do not believe.
³⁷All that the Father gives me will come to me,
and whoever comes to me
I shall not turn him away;
³⁸because I have come from heaven,
not to do my own will,
but to do the will of the one who sent me.
³⁹Now the will of him who sent me
is that I should lose nothing
of all that he has given to me,
and that I should raise it up on the last day.
⁴⁰Yes, it is my Father's will
that whoever sees the Son and believes in him
shall have eternal life,
and that I shall raise him up on the last day.'

⁴¹Meanwhile the Jews were complaining to each other about him, because he had said, 'I am the bread that came down from heaven'. ⁴²'Surely this is Jesus son of Joseph' they said. 'We know his father and mother. How can he now say, "I have come down from heaven"?' ⁴³Jesus said in reply, 'Stop complaining to each other.

⁴⁴'No one can come to me
unless he is drawn by the Father who sent me,
and I will raise him up at the last day.
⁴⁵It is written in the prophets:

They will all be taught by God,[b]
and to hear the teaching of the Father,
and learn from it,
is to come to me.
[46]Not that anybody has seen the Father,
except the one who comes from God:
he has seen the Father.
[47]I tell you most solemnly,
everybody who believes has eternal life.
[48]I am the bread of life.
[49]Your fathers ate the manna in the desert
and they are dead;
[50]but this is the bread that comes down from heaven,
so that a man may eat it and not die.
[51]I am the living bread which has come down from heaven.
Anyone who eats this bread will live for ever;
and the bread that I shall give
is my flesh, for the life of the world.'

[52]Then the Jews started arguing with one another: 'How can this man give us his flesh to eat?' they said. [53]Jesus replied:

I tell you most solemnly,
if you do not eat the flesh of the Son of Man
and drink his blood,
you will not have life in you.
[54]Anyone who does eat my flesh and drink my blood
has eternal life,

---

[b]. Is 54:13

and I shall raise him up on the last day.

⁵⁵For my flesh is real food

and my blood is real drink.

⁵⁶He who eats my flesh and drinks my blood

lives in me and I live in him.

⁵⁷As I, who am sent by the living Father,

myself draw life from the Father,

so whoever eats me will draw life from me.

⁵⁸This is the bread come down from heaven;

not like the bread our ancestors ate:

they are dead,

but anyone who eats this bread will live for ever.'

⁵⁹He taught this doctrine at Capernaum, in the synagogue. ⁶⁰After hearing it, many of his followers said, 'This is intolerable language. How could anyone accept it?' ⁶¹Jesus was aware that his followers were complaining about it and said, 'Does this upset you? ⁶²What if you should see the Son of Man ascend to where he was before?

⁶³'It is the spirit that gives life,

the flesh has nothing to offer.

The words I have spoken to you are spirit

and they are life.

⁶⁴'But there are some of you who do not believe.' For Jesus knew from the outset those who did not believe, and who it was that would betray him. ⁶⁵He went on, 'This is why I told you that no one could come to me

unless the Father allows him'. ⁶⁶After this, many of his disciples left him and stopped going with him.

Peter's profession of faith

⁶⁷Then Jesus said to the Twelve, 'What about you, do you want to go away too?' ⁶⁸Simon Peter answered, 'Lord, who shall we go to? You have the message of eternal life, ⁶⁹and we believe; we know that you are the Holy One of God.' ⁷⁰Jesus replied, 'Have I not chosen you, you Twelve? Yet one of you is a devil.' ⁷¹He meant Judas son of Simon Iscariot, since this was the man, one of the Twelve, who was going to betray him.

V. THE FEAST OF TABERNACLES

Jesus goes up to Jerusalem for the feast and teaches there

7 ¹After this Jesus stayed in Galilee; he could not stay in Judaea, because the Jews were out to kill him.

²As the Jewish feast of Tabernacles drew near, ³his brothers[a] said to him, 'Why not leave this place and go to Judaea, and let your disciples[b] see the works you are doing; ⁴if a man wants to be known he does not do things in secret; since you are doing all this, you should let the whole world see'. ⁵Not even his brothers, in fact, had faith in him. ⁶Jesus answered, 'The right time for me has

---

[7a.] In the wide sense, as in Mt 12:46: relations of his own generation.

[7b.] Those in Jerusalem and Judaea.

not come yet, but any time is the right time for you. [7]The world cannot hate you, but it does hate me, because I give evidence that its ways are evil. [8]Go up to the festival yourselves: I am not going to this festival, because for me the time is not ripe yet.' [9]Having said that, he stayed behind in Galilee.

[10]However, after his brothers had left for the festival, he went up as well, but quite privately, without drawing attention to himself. [11]At the festival the Jews were on the look-out for him: 'Where is he?' they said. [12]People stood in groups whispering[c] about him. Some said, 'He is a good man'; others, 'No, he is leading the people astray'. [13]Yet no one spoke about him openly, for fear of the Jews.

[14]When the festival was half over, Jesus went to the Temple and began to teach. [15]The Jews were astonished and said, 'How did he learn to read? He has not been taught.' [16]Jesus answered them:

'My teaching is not from myself:
it comes from the one who sent me;
[17]and if anyone is prepared to do his will,
he will know whether my teaching is from God
or whether my doctrine is my own.
[18]When a man's doctrine is his own
he is hoping to get honour for himself;
but when he is working for the honour of one who sent him,
then he is sincere

[7c.] Or 'In the crowds there was whispering about him'.

and by no means an impostor.

[19]Did not Moses give you the Law?

And yet not one of you keeps the Law!

'Why do you want to kill me?' [20]The crowd replied, 'You are mad! Who wants to kill you?' [21]Jesus answered, 'One work I did, and you are all surprised by it. [22]Moses ordered you to practise circumcision - not that it began with him, it goes back to the patriarchs - and you circumcise on the sabbath. [23]Now if a man can be circumcised on the sabbath so that the Law of Moses is not broken, why are you angry with me for making a man whole and complete on a sabbath? [24]Do not keep judging according to appearances; let your judgement be according to what is right.'

The people discuss the origin of the Messiah

[25]Meanwhile some of the people of Jerusalem were saying, 'Isn't this the man they want to kill? [26]And here he is, speaking freely, and they have nothing to say to him! Can it be true the authorities have made up their minds that he is the Christ? [27]Yet we all know where he comes from, but when the Christ appears no one will know where he comes from.'[d]

[28]Then, as Jesus taught in the Temple, he cried out:

'Yes, you know me and you know where I came from.

[7 d.] Although the prophecy that the Messiah would be born in Bethlehem was well known, it was commonly believed that he would appear suddenly from some secret place.

Yet I have not come of myself:
no, there is one who sent me and I really come from him,
and you do not know him,
[29]but I know him
because I have come from him
and it was he who sent me.'

[30]They would have arrested him then, but because his time had not yet come no one laid a hand on him.

Jesus foretells his approaching departure

[31]There were many people in the crowds, however, who believed in him; they were saying, 'When the Christ comes, will he give more signs than this man?' [32]Hearing that rumours like this about him were spreading among the people, the Pharisees sent the Temple police to arrest him. [33]Then Jesus said:

'I shall remain with you for only a short time now;
then I shall go back to the one who sent me.
[34]You will look for me and will not find me:
where I am,
you cannot come.'

[35]The Jews then said to one another, 'Where is he going that we shan't be able to find him? Is he going abroad to the people who are dispersed among the Greeks and will he teach the Greeks? [36]What does he mean when he says:

"You will look for me and will not find me:
where I am,
you cannot come"?'

The promise of living water

³⁷On the last day and greatest day of the festival, Jesus stood there and cried out:

'If any man is thirsty, let him come to me!

Let the man come and drink ³⁸who believes in me!'

As scripture says: From his breast shall flow fountains of living water.ᵉ

³⁹He was speaking of the Spirit which those who believed in him were to receive; for there was no Spirit as yet because Jesus had not yet been glorified.

Fresh discussions on the origin of the Messiah

⁴⁰Several people who had been listening said, 'Surely he must be the prophet', ⁴¹and some said, 'He is the Christ', but others said, 'Would the Christ be from Galilee? ⁴²Does not scripture say that the Christ must be descended from David and come from the town of Bethlehem?' ⁴³So the people could not agree about him. ⁴⁴Some would have liked to arrest him, but no one actually laid hands on him.

⁴⁵The police went back to the chief priests and Pharisees who said to them, 'Why haven't you brought him?' ⁴⁶The police replied, 'There has never been anybody who has spoken like him'. ⁴⁷'So' the Pharisees answered 'you have been led astray as well? ⁴⁸Have any

---

⁷ᵉ· Life-giving water for Zion was a theme of the readings from scripture on the feast of Tabernacles (Zc 14:8, Ezk 47:1f); the liturgy included prayers for rain and the commemoration of the miracle of Moses and the water, Ex 17.

of the authorities believed in him? Any of the Pharisees?
⁴⁹This rabble knows nothing about the Law - they are
damned.' ⁵⁰One of them, Nicodemus - the same man who
had come to Jesus earlier - said to them, ⁵¹'But surely the
Law does not allow us to pass judgement on a man
without giving him a hearing and discovering what he is
about?' ⁵²To this they answered, 'Are you a Galilean too?
Go into the matter, and see for yourself: prophets do not
come out of Galilee.'

The adulterous woman[f]

They all went home, **8**¹and Jesus went to the Mount of
Olives.

²At daybreak he appeared in the Temple again; and as all
the people came to him, he sat down and began to teach them.

³The scribes and Pharisees brought a woman along
who had been caught committing adultery; and making
her stand there in full view of everybody, ⁴they said to
Jesus, 'Master, this woman was caught in the very act of
committing adultery, ⁵and Moses has ordered us in the
Law to condemn women like this to death by stoning.
What have you to say?' ⁶They asked him this as a test,
looking for something to use against him. But Jesus bent
down and started writing on the ground with his finger.
⁷As they persisted with their question, he looked up and

[7f.] The author of this passage is not John; the oldest MSS do not include
it or place it elsewhere. The style is that of the Synoptics.

said, 'If there is one of you who has not sinned, let him be the first to throw a stone at her'. [8]Then he bent down and wrote on the ground again. [9]When they heard this they went away one by one, beginning with the eldest, until Jesus was left alone with the woman, who remained standing there. [10]He looked up and said, 'Woman, where are they? Has no one condemned you?' [11]'No one, sir' she replied. 'Neither do I condemn you,' said Jesus 'go away, and don't sin any more.'

Jesus, the light of the world

[12]When Jesus spoke to the people again, he said:

'I am the light of the world;
anyone who follows me will not be walking in the dark;
he will have the light of life'.

A discussion on the testimony of Jesus to himself

[13]At this the Pharisees said to him, 'You are testifying on your own behalf; your testimony is not valid'. [14]Jesus replied:

'It is true that I am testifying on my own behalf,
but my testimony is still valid,
because I know
where I came from and where I am going;
but you do not know
where I come from or where I am going.
[15]You judge by human standards;
I judge no one,
[16]but if I judge,

my judgement will be sound,

because I am not alone:

the one who sent me is with me;

¹⁷and in your Law it is written

that the testimony of two witnesses is valid.

¹⁸I may be testifying on my own behalf,

but the Father who sent me is my witness too.'

¹⁹They asked him, 'Where is your Father?' Jesus answered:

'You do not know me, nor do you know my Father;

if you did know me, you would know my Father as well'.

²⁰He spoke these words in the Treasury, while teaching in the Temple. No one arrested him, because his time had not yet come.

The unbelieving Jews warned

²¹Again he said to them:

'I am going away; you will look for me

and you will die in your sin.

Where I am going, you cannot come.'

²²The Jews said to one another, 'Will he kill himself? Is that what he means by saying, "Where I am going, you cannot come"?' ²³Jesus went on:

'You are from below;

I am from above.

You are of this world;

I am not of this world.

²⁴I have told you already: You will die in your sins.

Yes, if you do not believe that I am He,
you will die in your sins.'

²⁵So they said to him, 'Who are you?' Jesus answered:

'What I have told you from the outset.
²⁶About you I have much to say
and much to condemn;
but the one who sent me is truthful,
and what I have learnt from him
I declare to the world.'

²⁷They failed to understand that he was talking to them
about the Father. ²⁸So Jesus said:

'When you have lifted up the Son of Man,
then you will know that I am He
and that I do nothing of myself:
what the Father has taught me
is what I preach;
²⁹he who sent me is with me,
and has not left me to myself,
for I always do what pleases him'.

³⁰As he was saying this, many came to believe in him.

Jesus and Abraham

³¹To the Jews who believed in him Jesus said:

'If you make my word your home
you will indeed be my disciples,
³²you will learn the truth
and the truth will make you free'.

³³They answered, 'We are descended from Abraham and

we have never been the slaves of anyone; what do you
mean, "You will be made free"?' [34]Jesus replied:

'I tell you most solemnly,
everyone who commits sin is a slave.
[35]Now the slave's place in the house is not assured,
but the son's place is assured.
[36]So if the Son makes you free,
you will be free indeed.
[37]I know that you are descended from Abraham;
but in spite of that you want to kill me
because nothing I say has penetrated into you.
[38]What I, for my part, speak of
is what I have seen with my Father;
but you, you put into action
the lessons learnt from your father.'

[39]They repeated, 'Our father is Abraham'. Jesus said to them:

'If you were Abraham's children,
you would do as Abraham did.
[40]As it is, you want to kill me
when I tell you the truth
as I have learnt it from God;
that is not what Abraham did.
[41]What you are doing is what your father does.'

'We were not born of prostitution,'[a] they went on 'we
have one father: God.' [42]Jesus answered:

[8a.] By 'prostitution' the prophets often mean religious infidelity, cf.
Ho 1:2.

'If God were your father, you would love me,
since I have come here from God;
     yes, I have come from him;
not that I came because I chose,
no, I was sent, and by him.
[43]Do you know why you cannot take in what I say?
It is because you are unable to understand my language.
[44]The devil is your father,
and you prefer to do
what your father wants.

He was a murderer from the start;
he was never grounded in the truth;
there is no truth in him at all:
when he lies
he is drawing on his own store,
because he is a liar, and the father of lies.
[45]But as for me, I speak the truth
and for that very reason,
you do not believe me.
[46]Can one of you convict me of sin?
If I speak the truth, why do you not believe me?
[47]A child of God
listens to the words of God;
if you refuse to listen,
it is because you are not God's children.'
[48]The Jews replied, 'Are we not right in saying that you are

a Samaritan and possessed by a devil?' Jesus answered:

⁴⁹'I am not possessed;
no, I honour my Father,
but you want to dishonour me.
⁵⁰Not that I care for my own glory,
there is someone who takes care of that
    and is the judge of it.
⁵¹I tell you most solemnly,
whoever keeps my word
will never see death.'

⁵²The Jews said, 'Now we know for certain that you are possessed. Abraham is dead, and the prophets are dead, and yet you say, "Whoever keeps my word will never know the taste of death". ⁵³Are you greater than our father Abraham, who is dead? The prophets are dead too. Who are you claiming to be?' ⁵⁴Jesus answered:

'If I were to seek my own glory
that would be no glory at all;
my glory is conferred by the Father,
by the one of whom you say, "He is our God"
⁵⁵although you do not know him.
But I know him,
and if I were to say: I do not know him,
I should be a liar, as you are liars yourselves.
But I do know him, and I faithfully keep his word.
⁵⁶Your father Abraham rejoiced
to think that he would see my Day;

he saw it and was glad.'

[57]The Jews then said, 'You are not fifty yet, and you have seen Abraham!' [58]Jesus replied:

'I tell you most solemnly,

before Abraham ever was,

I Am'.

[59]At this they picked up stones to throw at him[b]; but Jesus hid himself and left the Temple.

The cure of the man born blind

9 [1]As he went along, he saw a man who had been blind from birth. [2]His disciples asked him, 'Rabbi, who sinned, this man or his parents, for him to have been born blind?' [3]'Neither he nor his parents sinned,' Jesus answered 'he was born blind so that the works of God might be displayed in him.

[4]'As long as the day lasts

I must carry out the work of the one who sent me;

the night will soon be here when no one can work.

[5]As long as I am in the world

I am the light of the world.'

[6]Having said this, he spat on the ground, made a paste with the spittle, put this over the eyes of the blind man, [7]and said to him, 'Go and wash in the Pool of Siloam[a] (a name that means 'sent'). So the blind man went off and

---

[8 b.] Stoning was the penalty for blasphemy. Cf. 10:33.

[9 a.] Water from this pool was drawn during the feast of Tabernacles to symbolise the waters of blessing.

washed himself, and came away with his sight restored.

⁸His neighbours and people who earlier had seen him begging said, 'Isn't this the man who used to sit and beg?' ⁹Some said, 'Yes, it is the same one'. Others said, 'No, he only looks like him'. The man himself said, 'I am the man'. ¹⁰So they said to him, 'Then how do your eyes come to be open?' ¹¹'The man called Jesus' he answered 'made a paste, daubed my eyes with it and said to me, "Go and wash at Siloam"; so I went, and when I washed I could see.' ¹²They asked, 'Where is he?' 'I don't know' he answered.

¹³They brought the man who had been blind to the Pharisees. ¹⁴It had been a sabbath day when Jesus made the paste and opened the man's eyes, ¹⁵so when the Pharisees asked him how he had come to see, he said, 'He put a paste on my eyes, and I washed, and I can see'. ¹⁶Then some of the Pharisees said, 'This man cannot be from God: he does not keep the sabbath'. Others said, 'How could a sinner produce signs like this?' And there was disagreement among them. ¹⁷So they spoke to the blind man again, 'What have you to say about him yourself, now that he has opened your eyes?' 'He is a prophet' replied the man.

¹⁸However, the Jews would not believe that the man had been blind and had gained his sight, without first sending for his parents and ¹⁹asking them, 'Is this man really your son who you say was born blind? If so, how is it that he is now able to see?' ²⁰His parents answered, 'We know he is our son and we know he was born blind,

²¹but we don't know how it is that he can see now, or who opened his eyes. He is old enough: let him speak for himself.' ²²His parents spoke like this out of fear of the Jews, who had already agreed to expel from the synagogue anyone who should acknowledge Jesus as the Christ. ²³This was why his parents said, 'He is old enough; ask him'.

²⁴So the Jews again sent for the man and said to him, 'Give glory to God!ᵇ For our part, we know that this man is a sinner.' ²⁵The man answered, 'I don't know if he is a sinner; I only know that I was blind and now I can see'. ²⁶They said to him, 'What did he do to you? How did he open your eyes?' ²⁷He replied, 'I have told you once and you wouldn't listen. Why do you want to hear it all again? Do you want to become his disciples too?' ²⁸At this they hurled abuse at him: 'You can be his disciple,' they said 'we are disciples of Moses: ²⁹we know that God spoke to Moses, but as for this man, we don't know where he comes from'. ³⁰The man replied, 'Now here is an astonishing thing! He has opened my eyes, and you don't know where he comes from! ³¹We know that God doesn't listen to sinners, but God does listen to men who are devout and do his will. ³²Ever since the world began it is unheard of for anyone to open the eyes of a man who was born blind; ³³if this man were not from God, he couldn't do a thing.' ³⁴'Are you trying to teach us,' they

⁹ᵇ i.e. putting the man on oath.

replied 'and you a sinner through and through, since you were born!' And they drove him away.

³⁵Jesus heard they had driven him away, and when he found him he said to him, 'Do you believe in the Son of Man?' ³⁶'Sir,' the man replied 'tell me who he is so that I may believe in him.' ³⁷Jesus said, 'You are looking at him; he is speaking to you'. ³⁸The man said, 'Lord, I believe', and worshiped him. ³⁹Jesus said:

'It is for judgement
that I have come into this world,
so that those without sight may see
and those with sight turn blind'.

⁴⁰Hearing this, some Pharisees who were present said to him, 'We are not blind, surely?' ⁴¹Jesus replied:

'Blind? If you were,
you would not be guilty,
but since you say, "We see",
your guilt remains.

The good shepherd

10 ¹'I tell you most solemnly, anyone who does not enter the sheepfold through the gate, but gets in some other way is a thief and a brigand. ²The one who enters through the gate is the shepherd of the flock; ³the gatekeeper lets him in, the sheep hear his voice, one by one he calls his own sheep and leads them out. ⁴When he has brought out his flock, he goes ahead of them, and the sheep follow because they know his voice. ⁵They never follow a stranger but run away from him: they do not recognise the voice of strangers.'

⁶Jesus told them[a] this parable but they failed to understand what he meant by telling it to them.

⁷So Jesus spoke to them again:

'I tell you most solemnly,
I am the gate of the sheepfold.
⁸All others who have come
are thieves and brigands;
but the sheep took no notice of them.
⁹I am the gate.
Anyone who enters through me will be safe:
he will go freely in and out
and be sure of finding pasture.
¹⁰The thief comes
only to steal and kill and destroy.
I have come
so that they may have life
and have it to the full.
¹¹I am the good shepherd:
the good shepherd is one who lays down his life
for his sheep.
¹²The hired man, since he is not the shepherd
and the sheep do not belong to him,
abandons the sheep and runs away
as soon as he sees a wolf coming,

---

10 a. The Pharisees.

and then the wolf attacks and scatters the sheep;
[13]this is because he is only a hired man
and has no concern for the sheep.
[14]I am the good shepherd;
I know my own
and my own know me,
[15]just as the Father knows me
and I know the Father;
and I lay down my life for my sheep.
[16]And there are other sheep I have
that are not of this fold,
and these I have to lead as well.
They too will listen to my voice,
and there will be only one flock,
and one shepherd.
[17]The Father loves me,
because I lay down my life
in order to take it up again.
[18]No one takes it from me;
I lay it down of my own free will,
and as it is in my power to lay it down,
so it is in my power to take it up again;
and this is the command I have been given by my Father.'
[19]These words caused disagreement among the Jews. [20]Many said, 'He is possessed, he is raving; why bother to listen to him?' [21]Others said, 'These are not the words of a man possessed by a devil: could a devil open the eyes of the blind?'

VI. THE FEAST OF DEDICATION

Jesus claims to be the Son of God

²²It was the time when the feast of Dedication was being celebrated in Jerusalem. It was winter, ²³and Jesus was in the Temple walking up and down in the Portico of Solomon. ²⁴The Jews gathered round him and said, 'How much longer are you going to keep us in suspense? If you are the Christ, tell us plainly.' ²⁵Jesus replied:

'I have told you, but you do not believe.

The works I do in my Father's name are my witness;

²⁶but you do not believe,

because you are no sheep of mine.

²⁷The sheep that belong to me listen to my voice;

I know them and they follow me.

²⁸I give them eternal life;

they will never be lost

and no one will ever steal them from me.

²⁹The Father who gave them to me is greater than anyone,

and no one can steal from the Father.

³⁰The Father and I are one.'

³¹The Jews fetched stones to stone him, ³²so Jesus said to them, 'I have done many good works for you to see, works from my Father; for which of these are you stoning me?' ³³The Jews answered him, 'We are not stoning you for doing a good work but for blasphemy: you are only a man and you claim to be God.' ³⁴Jesus answered:

'Is it not written in your Law:
I said, you are gods?[b]

³⁵So the Law uses the word gods
of those to whom the word of God was addressed,
and scripture cannot be rejected.
³⁶Yet you say to someone the Father has consecrated
         and sent into the world,
"You are blaspheming",
because he says, "I am the son of God".
³⁷If I am not doing my Father's work,
there is no need to believe me;
³⁸but if I am doing it,
then even if you refuse to believe in me,
at least believe in the work I do;
then you will know for sure
that the Father is in me and I am in the Father.'
³⁹They wanted to arrest him then, but he eluded them.

Jesus withdraws to the other side of the Jordan
⁴⁰He went back again to the far side of the Jordan to stay
in the district where John had once been baptising.
⁴¹Many people who came to him there said, 'John gave no
signs, but all he said about this man was true'; ⁴²and many
of them believed in him.

---

¹⁰ᵇ Ps 82:6

The resurrection of Lazarus

11 ¹There was a man named Lazarus who lived in the village of Bethany with the two sisters, Mary and Martha, and he was ill. - ²It was the same Mary, the sister of the sick man Lazarus, who anointed the Lord with ointment and wiped his feet with her hair. ³The sisters sent this message to Jesus, 'Lord, the man you love is ill'. ⁴On receiving the message, Jesus said, 'This sickness will end not in death but in God's glory, and through it the Son of God will be glorified'.

⁵Jesus loved Martha and her sister and Lazarus, ⁶yet when he heard that Lazarus was ill he stayed where he was for two more days ⁷before saying to the disciples, 'Let us go to Judaea'. ⁸The disciples said, 'Rabbi, it is not long since the Jews wanted to stone you; are you going back again?' ⁹Jesus replied:

'Are there not twelve hours in the day?

A man can walk in the daytime without stumbling

because he has the light of this world to see by;

¹⁰but if he walks at night he stumbles,

because there is no light to guide him.'

¹¹He said that and then added, 'Our friend Lazarus is resting, I am going to wake him'. ¹²The disciples said to him, 'Lord, if he is able to rest he is sure to get better'. ¹³The phrase Jesus used referred to the death of Lazarus, but they thought that by 'rest' he meant 'sleep', so ¹⁴Jesus put it plainly, 'Lazarus is dead; ¹⁵and for your sake I am

glad I was not there because now you will believe. But let us go to him.' [16]Then Thomas - known as the Twin - said to the other disciples, 'Let us go too, and die with him'.

[17]On arriving, Jesus found that Lazarus had been in the tomb for four days already. [18]Bethany is only about two miles from Jerusalem, [19]and many Jews had come to Martha and Mary to sympathise with them over their brother. [20]When Martha heard that Jesus had come she went to meet him. Mary remained sitting in the house. [21]Martha said to Jesus, 'If you had been here, my brother would not have died, [22]but I know that, even now, whatever you ask of God, he will grant you'. [23]'Your brother' said Jesus to her 'will rise again.' [24]Martha said, 'I know he will rise again at the resurrection on the last day'. [25]Jesus said:

'I am the resurrection.

If anyone believes in me, even though he dies he will live,

[26]and whoever lives and believes in me

will never die.

Do you believe this?'

[27]'Yes, Lord,' she said 'I believe that you are the Christ, the Son of God, the one who was to come into this world.'

[28]When she had said this, she went and called her sister Mary, saying in a low voice, 'The Master is here and wants to see you'. [29]Hearing this, Mary got up quickly and went to him. [30]Jesus had not yet come into the village; he was still at the place where Martha had met him. [31]When the Jews who were in the house sympathising with Mary

saw her get up so quickly and go out, they followed her, thinking that she was going to the tomb to weep there.

³²Mary went to Jesus, and as soon as she saw him she threw herself at his feet, saying, 'Lord, if you had been here, my brother would not have died'. ³³At the sight of her tears, and those of the Jews who followed her, Jesus said in great distress, with a sigh that came straight from the heart, ³⁴'Where have you put him?' They said, 'Lord, come and see'. ³⁵Jesus wept; ³⁶and the Jews said, 'See how much he loved him!' ³⁷But there were some who remarked, 'He opened the eyes of the blind man, could he not have prevented this man's death?' ³⁸Still sighing, Jesus reached the tomb: it was a cave with a stone to close the opening. ³⁹Jesus said, 'Take the stone away'. Martha said to him, 'Lord, by now he will smell; this is the fourth day'. ⁴⁰Jesus replied, 'Have I not told you that if you believe you will see the glory of God?' ⁴¹So they took away the stone. Then Jesus lifted up his eyes and said:

'Father, I thank you for hearing my prayer.
⁴²I knew indeed that you always hear me,
 but I speak
 for the sake of all these who stand round me,
  so that they may believe it was you who sent me.'
⁴³When he had said this, he cried in a loud voice, 'Lazarus, here! Come out!' ⁴⁴The dead man came out, his feet and hands bound with bands of stuff and a cloth round his face. Jesus said to them, 'Unbind him, let him go free'.

The Jewish leaders decide on the death of Jesus

[45]Many of the Jews who had come to visit Mary and had seen what he did believed in him, [46]but some of them went to tell the Pharisees what Jesus had done. [47]Then the chief priests and Pharisees called a meeting. 'Here is this man working all these signs' they said 'and what action are we taking? [48]If we let him go on in this way everybody will believe in him, and the Romans will come and destroy the Holy Place and our nation.' [49]One of them, Caiaphas, the high priest that year, said, 'You don't seem to have grasped the situation at all; [50]you fail to see that it is better for one man to die for the people, than for the whole nation to be destroyed'. [51]He did not speak in his own person, it was as high priest that he made this prophecy that Jesus was to die for the nation - [52]and not for the nation only, but to gather together in unity the scattered children of God. [53]From that day they were determined to kill him. [54]So Jesus no longer went about openly among the Jews, but left the district for a town called Ephraim, in the country bordering on the desert, and stayed there with his disciples.

VII. THE LAST PASSOVER

A. Before the Passion

The Passover draws near

[55]The Jewish Passover drew near, and many of the country people who had gone up to Jerusalem to purify themselves [56]looked out for Jesus, saying to one another as they stood about in the Temple, 'What do you think? Will he come to

the festival or not?' ⁵⁷The chief priests and Pharisees had by now given their orders: anyone who knew where he was must inform them so that they could arrest him.

The anointing at Bethany

12 ¹Six days before the Passover, Jesus went to Bethany, where Lazarus was, whom he had raised from the dead. ²They gave a dinner for him there; Martha waited on them and Lazarus was among those at table. ³Mary brought in a pound of very costly ointment, pure nard, and with it anointed the feet of Jesus, wiping them with her hair; the house was full of the scent of the ointment. ⁴Then Judas Iscariot - one of his disciples, the man who was to betray him - said, ⁵'Why wasn't this ointment sold for three hundred denarii, and the money given to the poor?' ⁶He said this, not because he cared about the poor, but because he was a thief; he was in charge of the common fund and used to help himself to the contributions. ⁷So Jesus said, 'Leave her alone; she had to keep this scent for the day of my burial. ⁸You have the poor with you always, you will not always have me.'

⁹Meanwhile a large number of Jews heard that he was there and came not only on account of Jesus but also to see Lazarus whom he had raised from the dead. ¹⁰Then the chief priests decided to kill Lazarus as well, ¹¹since it was on his account that many of the Jews were leaving them and believing in Jesus.

The Messiah enters Jerusalem

¹²The next day the crowds who had come up for the festival heard that Jesus was on his way to Jerusalem. ¹³They took branches of palm and went out to meet him, shouting, '*Hosanna! Blessings on* the King of Israel, *who comes in the name of the Lord.*'ᵃ ¹⁴Jesus found a young donkey and mounted it - as scripture says: ¹⁵*Do not be afraid, daughter of Zion; see, your king is coming, mounted on the colt of a donkey.*ᵇ ¹⁶At the time his disciples did not understand this, but later, after Jesus had been glorified, they remembered that this had been written about him and that this was in fact how they had received him. ¹⁷All who had been with him when he called Lazarus out of the tomb and raised him from the dead were telling how they had witnessed it; ¹⁸it was because of this, too, that the crowd came out to meet him: they had heard that he had given this sign. ¹⁹Then the Pharisees said to one another, 'You see, there is nothing you can do; look, the whole world is running after him!'

Jesus foretells his death and subsequent glorification

²⁰Among those who went up to worship at the festival were some Greeks.ᶜ ²¹These approached Philip, who came from Bethsaida in Galilee, and put this request to him,

---

¹²ᵃ· Ps 118:26

¹²ᵇ· Zc 9:9f

¹²ᶜ· The 'God-fearing men' of Ac 10:2: converts who observed certain specific Mosaic observances.

'Sir, we should like to see Jesus'. ²²Philip went to tell Andrew, and Andrew and Philip together went to tell Jesus. ²³Jesus replied to them:

'Now the hour has come
for the Son of Man to be glorified.
²⁴I tell you, most solemnly,
unless a wheat grain falls on the ground and dies,
it remains only a single grain;
but if it dies,
it yields a rich harvest.
²⁵Anyone who loves his life loses it;
anyone who hates his life in this world
will keep it for the eternal life.
²⁶If a man serves me, he must follow me,
wherever I am, my servant will be there too.
If anyone serves me, my Father will honour him.
²⁷Now my soul is troubled.
What shall I say:
Father, save me from this hour?
But it was for this very reason that I have come to this hour.
²⁸Father, glorify your name!'

A voice came from heaven, 'I have glorified it, and I will glorify it again.' ²⁹People standing by, who heard this, said it was a clap of thunder; others said, 'It was an angel speaking to him'. ³⁰Jesus answered, 'It was not for my sake that this voice came, but for yours.

³¹'Now sentence is being passed on this world;

now the prince of this world is to be overthrown.[d]

³²And when I am lifted up from the earth,

I shall draw all men to myself.'

³³By these words he indicated the kind of death he would die. ³⁴The crowd answered, 'The Law has taught us that the Christ will remain for ever. How can you say, "The Son of Man must be lifted up"? Who is this Son of Man?' ³⁵Jesus then said:

'The light will be with you only a little longer now.

Walk while you have the light,

or the dark will overtake you;

he who walks in the dark does not know where he is going.

³⁶While you still have the light,

believe in the light

and you will become sons of light.'

Having said this, Jesus left them and kept himself hidden.

Conclusion: the unbelief of the Jews

³⁷Though they had been present when he gave so many signs, they did not believe in him; ³⁸this was to fulfil the words of the prophet Isaiah: *Lord, who could believe what we have heard said, and to whom has the power of the Lord been revealed?*[e] ³⁹Indeed, they were unable to believe because, as Isaiah says again: ⁴⁰*He has blinded their eyes, he has hardened their heart, for fear they*

---

12 d. Satan.

12 e. Is 53:1

should see with their eyes and understand with their heart, and turn to me for healing.[f]

[41]Isaiah said this when saw his glory,[g] and his words referred to Jesus. [42]And yet there were many who did believe in him, even among the leading men, but they did not admit it, through fear of the Pharisees and fear of being expelled from the synagogue: [43]they put honour from men before the honour that comes from God. [44]Jesus declared publicly:

'Whoever believes in me
believes not in me
but in the one who sent me,
[45]and whoever sees me,
sees the one who sent me.
[46]I, the light, have come into the world,
so that whoever believes in me
need not stay in the dark any more.
[47]If anyone hears my words and does not
      keep them faithfully,
it is not I who shall condemn him,
since I have come not to condemn the world,
but to save the world:
[48]he who rejects me and refuses my words
has his judge already:

---

12 f. Is 6:9f
12 g. Isaiah's vision in the Temple, Is 6:4, interpreted as a prophetic vision of Christ's glory.

66

the word itself that I have spoken
will be his judge on the last day.
[49]For what I have spoken does not come from myself;
no, what I was to say, what I had to speak,
was commanded by the Father who sent me,
[50]and I know that his commands mean eternal life.
And therefore what the Father has told me
is what I speak.'

B. The Last Supper

Jesus washes his disciples' feet

13 [1]It was before the festival of the Passover, and Jesus knew that the hour had come for him to pass from this world to the Father. He had always loved those who were his in the world, but now he showed how perfect his love was.

[2]They were at supper, and the devil had already put it into the mind of Judas Iscariot son of Simon, to betray him. [3]Jesus knew that the Father had put everything into his hands, and that he had come from God and was returning to God, [4]and he got up from table, removed his outer garment and, taking a towel, wrapped it round his waist; [5]he then poured water into a basin and began to wash the disciples' feet[a] and to wipe them with the towel he was wearing.

[6]He came to Simon Peter, who said to him, 'Lord, are you going to wash my feet?' [7]Jesus answered, 'At the moment

---

[13 a.] The dress and the duty are those of a slave.

67

you do not know what I am doing, but later you will understand'. [8]'Never!' said Peter 'You shall never wash my feet.' Jesus replied, 'If I do not wash you, you can have nothing in common with me'. [9]'Then, Lord,' said Simon Peter 'not only my feet, but my hands and my head as well!' [10]Jesus said, 'No one who has taken a bath needs washing, he is clean all over. You too are clean, though not all of you are.'

[11]He knew who was going to betray him, that was why he said, 'though not all of you are'. [12]When he had washed their feet and put on his clothes again he went back to the table. 'Do you understand' he said 'what I have done to you? [13]You call me Master and Lord, and rightly; so I am. [14]If I, then, the Lord and Master, have washed your feet, you should wash each other's feet. [15]I have given you an example so that you may copy what I have done to you.

[16]'I tell you most solemnly,

no servant is greater than his master,

no messenger is greater than the man who sent him.

[17]'Now that you know this, happiness will be yours if you behave accordingly. [18]I am not speaking about all of you: I know the ones I have chosen; but what scripture says must be fulfilled: *Someone who shares my table rebels against me.*[b]

[19]'I tell you this now, before it happens,

so that when it does happen

you may believe that I am He.

[20]I tell you most solemnly,

13 b. Ps 41:9

whoever welcomes the one I send welcomes me,
and whoever welcomes me welcomes the one who sent me.'

The treachery of Judas foretold

²¹Having said this, Jesus was troubled in spirit and declared, 'I tell you most solemnly, one of you will betray me'. ²²The disciples looked at one another, wondering which he meant. ²³The disciple Jesus loved was reclining next to Jesus; ²⁴Simon Peter signed to him and said, 'Ask who it is he means', ²⁵so leaning back on Jesus' breast he said, 'Who is it, Lord?' ²⁶'it is the one' replied Jesus 'to whom I give the piece of bread that I shall dip in the dish.' He dipped the piece of bread and gave it to Judas son of Simon Iscariot. ²⁷At that instant, after Judas had taken the bread, Satan entered him. Jesus then said, 'What you are going to do, do quickly'. ²⁸None of the others at table understood the reason he said this. ²⁹Since Judas had charge of the common fund, some of them thought Jesus was telling him, 'Buy what we need for the festival', or telling him to give something to the poor. ³⁰As soon as Judas had taken the piece of bread he went out. Night had fallen. ³¹When he had gone Jesus said:

'Now has the Son of Man been glorified,
and in him God has been glorified.
³²If God has been glorified in him,
God will in turn glorify him in himself,ᶜ
and will glorify him very soon.

---

¹³ᶜ· i.e. the Father will take the Son of Man to himself in glory.

Farewell discourses

³³'My little children,
I shall not be with you much longer.
You will look for me,
and, as I told the Jews,
where I am going,
you cannot come.
³⁴I give you a new commandment:
love one another;
just as I have loved you,
you also must love one another.
³⁵By this love you have for one another,
everyone will know that you are my disciples.'

³⁶Simon Peter said, 'Lord, where are you going?' Jesus replied, 'Where I am going you cannot follow me now; you will follow me later'. ³⁷Peter said to him, 'Why can't I follow you now? I will lay down my life for you.' ³⁸'Lay down your life for me?' answered Jesus. 'I tell you most solemnly, before the cock crows you will have disowned me three times.

14 ¹'Do not let your hearts be troubled.
Trust in God still, and trust in me.
²There are many rooms in my Father's house;
if there were not, I should have told you.
I am going now to prepare a place for you,
³and after I have gone and prepared you a place,
I shall return to take you with me;

so that where I am

you may be too.

⁴'You know the way to the place where I am going.'
⁵Thomas said, 'Lord, we do not know where you are
going, so how can we know the way?' ⁶Jesus said:

'I am the Way, the Truth and the Life.

No one can come to the Father except through me.

⁷If you know me, you know my Father too.

From this moment you know him and have seen him.'
⁸Philip said, 'Lord, let us see the Father and then we shall
be satisfied'. ⁹'Have I been with you all this time, Philip,'
said Jesus to him 'and you still do not know me?

'To have seen me is to have seen the Father,

so how can you say, "Let us see the Father"?

¹⁰Do you not believe

that I am in the Father and the Father is in me?

The words I say to you I do not speak as from myself:

it is the Father, living in me, who is doing this work.

¹¹You must believe me when I say

that I am in the Father and the Father is in me;

believe it on the evidence of this work, if for no other reason.

¹²I tell you most solemnly,

whoever believes in me

will perform the same works as I do myself,

he will perform even greater works,

because I am going to the Father.

¹³Whatever you ask for in my name I will do,

so that the Father may be glorified in the Son.
[14]If you ask for anything in my name,
I will do it.
[15]If you love me you will keep my commandments.
[16]I shall ask the Father,
and he will give you another Advocate[a]
to be with you for ever,
[17]that Spirit of truth
whom the world can never receive
since it neither sees nor knows him;
but you know him,
because he is with you, he is in you.
[18]I will not leave you orphans;
I will come back to you.
[19]In a short time the world will no longer see me;
but you will see me,
because I live and you will live.
[20]On that day
you will understand that I am in my Father
and you in me and I in you.
[21]Anybody who receives my commandments
        and keeps them
will be one who loves me;
and anybody who loves me will be loved by my Father,
and I shall love him and show myself to him.'

[14a.] Greek parakletos: advocate or counsellor or protector.

²²Judas^b - this was not Judas Iscariot - said to him, 'Lord, what is all this about? Do you intend to show yourself to us and not to the world?' ²³Jesus replied:

'If anyone loves me he will keep my word,
and my Father will love him,
and we shall come to him
and make our home with him.

²⁴Those who do not love me do not keep my words.
And my word is not my own:
it is the word of the one who sent me.

²⁵I have said these things to you
while still with you;

²⁶but the Advocate, the Holy Spirit,
whom the Father will send in my name,
will teach you everything
and remind you of all I have said to you.

²⁷Peace^c I bequeath to you,
my own peace I give you,
a peace the world cannot give, this is my gift to you.
Do not let your hearts be troubled or afraid.

²⁸You heard me say:
I am going away, and shall return.
If you loved me you would have been glad
      to know that I am going to the Father,

---

14 b. 'Judas, brother of James' in Lk 6:16 and Ac 1:13; the Thaddaeus of Mt 10:3 and Mk 3:18.

14 c. The customary Jewish farewell.

for the Father is greater than I.

²⁹I have told you this now before it happens,
so that when it does happen you may believe.
³⁰I shall not talk with you any longer,
because the prince of this world is on his way.
He has no power over me,
³¹but the world must be brought to know
        that I love the Father
and that I am doing exactly what the Father told me.
Come now, let us go.

The true vine

15 ¹'I am the true vine,
and my Father is the vinedresser.
²Every branch in me that bears no fruit
he cuts away,
and every branch that does bear fruit he prunes
to make it bear even more.
³You are pruned already,
by means of the word that I have spoken to you.
⁴Make your home in me, as I make mine in you.
As a branch cannot bear fruit all by itself,
but must remain part of the vine,
neither can you unless you remain in me.
⁵I am the vine,
you are the branches.
Whoever remains in me, with me in him,
bears fruit in plenty;

for cut off from me you can do nothing.
6Anyone who does not remain in me
is like a branch that has been thrown away
- he withers;
these branches are collected and thrown on the fire,
and they are burnt.
7If you remain in me
and my words remain in you,
you may ask what you will
and you shall get it.
8It is to the glory of my Father that you should
        bear much fruit,
and then you will be my disciples.
9As the Father has loved me,
so I have loved you.
Remain in my love,
10If you keep my commandments
you will remain in my love,
just as I have kept my Father's commandments
and remain in his love.
11I have told you this
so that my own joy may be in you
and your joy be complete.
12This is my commandment:
love one another,
as I have loved you.
13A man can have no greater love

than to lay down his life for his friends.
[14]You are my friends,
if you do what I command you.
[15]I shall not call you servants any more,
because a servant does not know
his master's business;
I call you friends,
because I have made known to you
everything I have learnt from my Father.
[16]You did not choose me,
no, I chose you;
and I commissioned you
to go out and to bear fruit,
fruit that will last;
and then the Father will give you
anything you ask him in my name.
[17]What I command you
is to love one another.

The hostile world

[18]'If the world hates you,
remember that it hated me before you.
[19]If you belonged to the world,
the world would love you as its own;
but because you do not belong to the world,
because my choice withdrew you from the world,
therefore the world hates you.
[20]Remember the words I said to you:

A servant is not greater than his master.
If they persecuted me,
they will persecute you too;
if they kept my word,
they will keep yours as well.
²¹But it will be on my account that they will do all this,
because they do not know the one who sent me.
²²If I had not come,
if I had not spoken to them,
they would have been blameless;
but as it is they have no excuse for their sin.
²³Anyone who hates me hates my Father.
²⁴If I had not performed such works among them
as no one else has ever done,
they would be blameless;
but as it is, they have seen all this,
and still they hate both me and my Father.
²⁵But all this was only to fulfil the words
      written in their Law:
*They hated me for no reason.*ᵃ
²⁶When the Advocate comes,
whom I shall send to you from the Father,
the Spirit of truth who issues from the Father,
he will be my witness.
²⁷And you too will be witnesses,
because you have been with me from the outset.

15 a. Ps 35:19

16

¹'I have told you all this
that your faith may not be shaken.
²They will expel you from the synagogues,
and indeed the hour is coming
when anyone who kills you will think he is doing
a holy duty for God.
³They will do these things
because they have never known either the Father or myself.
⁴But I have told you all this,
so that when the time for it comes
you may remember that I told you.

The coming of the Advocate

'I did not tell you this from the outset,
because I was with you;
⁵but now I am going to the one who sent me.
Not one of you has asked, "Where are you going?"
⁶Yet you are sad at heart because I have told you this.
⁷Still, I must tell you the truth:
it is for your own good that I am going
because unless I go,
the Advocate will not come to you;
but if I do go,
I will send him to you.
⁸And when he comes,
he will show the world how wrong it was,
about sin,
and about who was in the right,

and about judgement:
⁹about sin:
proved by their refusal to believe in me;
¹⁰about who was in the right:
proved by my going to the Father
and your seeing me no more;
¹¹about judgement:
proved by the prince of this world being
      already condemned.
¹²I still have many things to say to you
but they would be too much for you now.
¹³But when the Spirit of truth comes
he will lead you to the complete truth,
since he will not be speaking as from himself
but will say only what he has learnt;
and he will tell you of the things to come.
¹⁴He will glorify me,
since all he tells you
will be taken from what is mine.
¹⁵Everything the Father has is mine;
that is why I said:
All he tells you
will be taken from what is mine.

Jesus to return very soon

¹⁶'In a short time you will no longer see me,
and then a short time later you will see me again.'
¹⁷Then some of his disciples said to one another, 'What

does he mean, "In a short time you will no longer see me, and then a short time later you will see me again" and, "I am going to the Father"? [18]What is this "short time"? We don't know what he means.' [19]Jesus knew that they wanted to question him, so he said, 'You are asking one another what I meant by saying: In a short time you will no longer see me, and then a short time later you will see me again.

[20]'I tell you most solemnly,
you will be weeping and wailing
while the world will rejoice;
you will be sorrowful,
but your sorrow will turn to joy.
[21]A woman in childbirth suffers,
because her time has come;
but when she has given birth to the child
    she forgets the suffering
in her joy that a man has been born into the world.
[22]So it is with you: you are sad now,
but I shall see you again, and your hearts will be full of joy,
and that joy no one shall take from you.
[23]When that day comes,
you will not ask me any questions.
I tell you most solemnly,
anything you ask for from the Father
he will grant in my name.
[24]Until now you have not asked for anything in my name.
Ask and you will receive,

and so your joy will be complete.
²⁵I have been telling you all this in metaphors,
the hour is coming
when I shall no longer speak to you in metaphors;
but tell' about the Father in plain words.
²⁶When that day comes
you will ask in my name;
and I do not say that I shall pray to the Father for you,
²⁷because the Father himself loves you
for loving me
and believing that I came from God.
²⁸I came from the Father and have come into the world
and now I leave the world to go to the Father.'

²⁹His disciples said, 'Now you are speaking plainly and not using metaphors! ³⁰Now we see that you know everything, and do not have to wait for questions to be put into words; because of this we believe that you came from God.' ³¹Jesus answered them:

'Do you believe at last?
³²Listen; the time will come - in fact it has come already - when you will be scattered, each going his own way
and leaving me alone.
And yet I am not alone,
because the Father is with me.
³³I have told you all this
so that you may find peace in me.
In the world you will have trouble,

but be brave:
I have conquered the world.'

The priestly prayer of Christ

17 After saying this, Jesus raised his eyes to heaven and said:

¹'Father, the hour has come:
glorify your Son
so that your Son may glorify you;
²and, through the power over all mankind[a]
     that you have given him,
let him give eternal life to all those you have
     entrusted to him.
³And eternal life is this:
to know you,
the only true God,
and Jesus Christ whom you have sent.
⁴I have glorified you on earth
and finished the work
that you gave me to do.
⁵Now, Father, it is time for you to glorify me
with that glory I had with you
before ever the world was.
⁶I have made your name known
to the men you took from the world to give me.
They were yours and you gave them to me,

---

17 a. Lit. 'all flesh'.

and they have kept your word.
⁷Now at last they know
that all you have given me comes indeed from you;
⁸for I have given them
the teaching you gave to me,
and they have truly accepted this, that I came from you,
and have believed that it was you who sent me.
⁹I pray for them;
I am not praying for the world
but for those you have given me,
because they belong to you:
¹⁰all I have is yours
and all you have is mine,
and in them I am glorified.
¹¹I am not in the world any longer,
but they are in the world,
and I am coming to you.
Holy Father,
keep those you have given me true to your name,
so that they may be one like us.
¹²While I was with them,
I kept those you had given me true to your name.
I have watched over them and not one is lost
except the one who chose to be lost,ᵇ
and this was to fulfil the scriptures.
¹³But now I am coming to you

---

¹⁷ᵇ. Lit. 'the son of perdition'.

and while still in the world I say these things
to share my joy with them to the full.
[14]I passed your word on to them,
and the world hated them,
because they belong to the world
no more than I belong to the world.
[15]I am not asking you to remove them from the world,
but to protect them from the evil one.
[16]They do not belong to the world
any more than I belong to the world.
[17]Consecrate them in the truth;
your word is truth.
[18]As you sent me into the world,
I have sent them into the world,
[19]and for their sake I consecrate myself
so that they too may be consecrated in truth.
[20]I pray not only for these,
but for those also
who through their words will believe in me.
[21]May they all be one.
Father, may they be one in us,
as you are in me and I am in you,
so that the world may believe it was you who sent me.
[22]I have given them the glory you gave to me,
that they may be one as we are one.
[23]With me in them and you in me,
may they be so completely one

that the world will realise that it was you who sent me
and that I have loved them as much as you loved me.
²⁴Father,
I want those you have given me
to be with me where I am,
so that they may always see the glory
you have given me
because you loved me
before the foundation of the world.
²⁵Father, Righteous One,
the world has not known you,
but I have known you,
and these have known
that you have sent me.
²⁶I have made your name known to them
and will continue to make it known,
so that the love with which you loved me may be in them,
and so that I may be in them.'

C. The Passion

The arrest of Jesus

18 ¹After he had said all this Jesus left with his disciples and crossed the Kedron valley. There was a garden there, and he went into it with his disciples. ²Judas the traitor knew the place well, since Jesus had often met his disciples there, ³and he brought the cohort[a] to

---

[18a.] A detachment from the Roman garrison in Jerusalem.

this place together with a detachment of guards sent by the chief priests and the Pharisees, all with lanterns and torches and weapons. [4]Knowing everything that was going to happen to him, Jesus then came forward and said, 'Who are you looking for?' [5]They answered, 'Jesus the Nazarene'. He said, 'I am he'. Now Judas the traitor was standing among them. [6]When Jesus said, 'I am he', they moved back and fell to the ground. [7]He asked them a second time, 'Who are you looking for?' They said, 'Jesus the Nazarene'. [8]'I have told you that I am he' replied Jesus. 'If I am the one you are looking for, let these others go.' [9]This was to fulfil the words he had spoken, 'Not one of those you gave me have I lost'.

[10]Simon Peter, who carried a sword, drew it and wounded the high priest's servant, cutting off his right ear. The servant's name was Malchus. [11]Jesus said to Peter, 'Put your sword back in its scabbard; am I not to drink the cup that the Father has given me?'

Jesus before Annas and Caiaphas. Peter disowns him
[12]The cohort and its captain and the Jewish guards seized Jesus and bound him. [13]They took him first to Annas, because Annas was the father-in-law of Caiaphas, who was high priest that year. [14]It was Caiaphas who had suggested to the Jews, 'It is better for one man to die for the people'.

[15]Simon Peter, with another disciple, followed Jesus. This disciple, who was known to the high priest, went with Jesus into the high priest's palace, [16]but Peter stayed

outside the door. So the other disciple, the one known to the high priest, went out, spoke to the woman who was keeping the door and brought Peter in. ¹⁷The maid on duty at the door said to Peter, 'Aren't you another of that man's disciples?' He answered, 'I am not'. ¹⁸Now it was cold, and the servants and guards had lit a charcoal fire and were standing there warming themselves; so Peter stood there too, warming himself with the others.

¹⁹The high priest questioned Jesus about his disciples and his teaching. ²⁰Jesus answered, 'I have spoken openly for all the world to hear; I have always taught in the synagogue and in the Temple where all the Jews meet together: I have said nothing in secret. ²¹But why ask me? Ask my hearers what I taught: they know what I said.' ²²At these words, one of the guards standing by gave Jesus a slap in the face, saying, 'Is that the way to answer the high priest?' ²³Jesus replied, 'If there is something wrong in what I said, point it out; but if there is no offence in it, why do you strike me?' ²⁴Then Annas sent him, still bound, to Caiaphas the high priest.

²⁵As Simon Peter stood there warming himself, someone said to him, 'Aren't you another of his disciples?' He denied it saying, 'I am not'. ²⁶One of the high priest's servants, a relation of the man whose ear Peter had cut off, said, 'Didn't I see you in the garden with him?' ²⁷Again Peter denied it; and at once a cock crew.

Jesus before Pilate

[28]They then led Jesus from the house of Caiaphas to the Praetorium.[b] It was now morning. They did not go into the Praetorium themselves or they would be defiled[c] and unable to eat the passover. [29]So Pilate came outside to them and said, 'What charge do you bring against this man?' They replied, [30]'If he were not a criminal, we should not be handing him over to you'. [31]Pilate said, 'Take him yourselves, and try him by your own Law'. The Jews answered, 'We are not allowed to put a man to death'. [32]This was to fulfil the words Jesus had spoken indicating the way he was going to die.

[33]So Pilate went back into the Praetorium and called Jesus to him, 'Are you the king of the Jews?' he asked. [34]Jesus replied, 'Do you ask this of your own accord, or have others spoken to you about me?' [35]Pilate answered, 'Am I a Jew? It is your own people and the chief priests who have handed you over to me: what have you done?' [36]Jesus replied, 'Mine is not a kingdom of this world; if my kingdom were of this world, my men would have fought to prevent my being surrendered to the Jews. But my kingdom is not of this kind.' [37]'So you are a king then?' said Pilate. 'It is you who say it' answered Jesus. 'Yes, I am a king. I was born for this, I came into the world for this: to bear witness to the truth; and all who are on the side of truth listen to my voice.' [38]'Truth?' said Pilate 'What is that?'; and with that he went

---

[18 b.] The judicial court of the Roman procurator.
[18 c.] By entering the house of a pagan. Cf. Lk 7:6.

out again to the Jews and said, 'I find no case against him.
³⁹But according to a custom of yours I should release one
prisoner at the Passover; would you like me, then, to release
the king of the Jews?' ⁴⁰At this they shouted: 'Not this man,'
they said 'but Barabbas'. Barabbas was a brigand.

19 ¹Pilate then had Jesus taken away and scourged;
²and after this, the soldiers twisted some thorns into
a crown and put it on his head, and dressed him in a
purple robe. ³They kept coming up to him and saying,
'Hail, king of the Jews!'; and they slapped him in the face.

⁴Pilate came outside again and said to them, 'Look, I am
going to bring him out to you to let you see that I find no
case'. ⁵Jesus then came out wearing the crown of thorns and
the purple robe. Pilate said, 'Here is the man'. ⁶When they
saw him the chief priests and the guards shouted, 'Crucify
him! Crucify him!' Pilate said, 'Take him yourselves and
crucify him: I can find no case against him'. ⁷'We have a
Law,' the Jews replied 'and according to that Law he ought
to die, because he has claimed to be the Son of God.'

⁸When Pilate heard them say this his fears increased.
⁹Re-entering the Praetorium, he said to Jesus, 'Where do
you come from?' But Jesus made no answer. ¹⁰Pilate then
said to him, 'Are you refusing to speak to me? Surely you
know I have power to release you and I have power to
crucify you?' ¹¹'You would have no power over me' replied
Jesus 'if it had not been given you from above; that is why
the one who handed me over to you has the greater guilt.'

Jesus is condemned to death

[12]From that moment Pilate was anxious to set him free, but the Jews shouted, 'If you set him free you are no friend of Caesar's; anyone who makes himself king is defying Caesar'. [13]Hearing these words, Pilate had Jesus brought out, and seated himself on the chair of judgement at a place called the Pavement, in Hebrew Gabbatha. [14]It was Passover Preparation Day, about the sixth hour.[a] 'Here is your king' said Pilate to the Jews. [15]'Take him away, take him away!' they said. 'Crucify him!' 'Do you want me to crucify your king?' said Pilate. The chief priests answered, 'We have no king except Caesar'. [16]So in the end Pilate handed him over to them to be crucified.

The crucifixion

They then took charge of Jesus, [17]and carrying his own cross he went out of the city to the place of the skull or, as it was called in Hebrew, Golgotha, [18]where they crucified him with two others, one on either side with Jesus in the middle. [19]Pilate wrote out a notice and had it fixed to the cross; it ran: 'Jesus the Nazarene, King of the Jews'. [20]This notice was read by many of the Jews, because the place where Jesus was crucified was not far from the city, and the writing was in Hebrew, Latin and Greek. [21]So the Jewish chief priests said to Pilate, 'You should not write "King of

[19a]. On Preparation Day, the Passover supper was made ready for eating after sunset. The sixth hour is midday, by which time all leaven had to be removed from the house; during the feast only unleavened bread was eaten.

the Jews", but "This man said: I am King of the Jews"'.
²²Pilate answered, 'What I have written, I have written'.

Christ's garments divided

²³When the soldiers had finished crucifying Jesus they took his clothing and divided it into four shares, one for each soldier. His undergarment was seamless, woven in one piece from neck to hem; ²⁴so they said to one another, 'Instead of tearing it, let's throw dice to decide who is to have it'. In this way the words of scripture were fulfilled:

They shared out my clothing among them.
*They cast lots for my clothes.*ᵇ

This is exactly what the soldiers did.

Jesus and his mother

²⁵Near the cross of Jesus stood his mother and his mother's sister, Mary the wife of Clopas, and Mary of Magdala. ²⁶Seeing his mother and the disciple he loved standing near her, Jesus said to his mother, 'Woman, this is your son. ²⁷Then to the disciple he said, 'This is your mother'. And from that moment the disciple made a place for her in his home.

The death of Jesus

²⁸After this, Jesus knew that everything had now been completed, and to fulfil the scripture perfectly he said:

*'I am thirsty'.*ᶜ

---

¹⁹ᵇ· Ps 22:18
¹⁹ᶜ· Ps 22:15

²⁹A jar-full of vinegar stood there, so putting a sponge soaked in the vinegar on a hyssop stick they held it up to his mouth. ³⁰After Jesus had taken the vinegar he said, 'It is accomplished'; and bowing his head he gave up his spirit.

The pierced Christ

³¹It was Preparation Day, and to prevent the bodies remaining on the cross during the sabbath - since that sabbath was a day of special solemnity - the Jews asked Pilate to have the legs broken[d] and the bodies taken away. ³²Consequently the soldiers came and broke the legs of the first man who had been crucified with him and then of the other. ³³When they came to Jesus, they found he was already dead, and so instead of breaking his legs ³⁴one of the soldiers pierced his side with a lance; and immediately there came out blood and water. ³⁵This is the evidence of one who saw it - trustworthy evidence, and he knows he speaks the truth - and he gives it so that you may believe as well. ³⁶Because all this happened to fulfil the words of scripture:

Not one bone of his will be broken;[e]

³⁷and again, in another place scripture says:

They will look on the one whom they have pierced.[f]

[19 d.] To hasten death.

[19 e.] Two texts are here combined: Ps 34:20 and Ex 12:46. The allusion is both to God protecting the good man, and to the ritual for preparing the Passover lamb.

[19 f.] Zc 12:10

The burial

[38]After this, Joseph of Arimathaea, who was a disciple of Jesus - though a secret one because he was afraid of the Jews - asked Pilate to let him remove the body of Jesus. Pilate gave permission, so they came and took it away. [39]Nicodemus came as well - the same one who had first come to Jesus at night-time - and he brought a mixture of myrrh and aloes, weighing about a hundred pounds. [40]They took the body of Jesus and wrapped it with the spices in linen cloths, following the Jewish burial custom. [41]At the place where he had been crucified there was a garden, and in this garden a new tomb in which no one had yet been buried. [42]Since it was the Jewish Day of Preparation and the tomb was near at hand, they laid Jesus there.

VIII. THE DAY OF CHRIST'S RESURRECTION

The empty tomb

20[1]It was very early on the first day of the week and still dark, when Mary of Magdala came to the tomb. She saw that the stone had been moved away from the tomb [2]and came running to Simon Peter and the other disciple, the one Jesus loved. 'They have taken the Lord out of the tomb' she said 'and we don't know where they have put him.'

[3]So Peter set out with the other disciple, to go to the tomb. [4]They ran together, but the other disciple, running faster than Peter, reached the tomb first; [5]he bent down and saw the linen cloths lying on the ground, but did not

go in. [6]Simon Peter who was following now came up, went right into the tomb, saw the linen cloths on the ground, [7]and also the cloth that had been over his head; this was not with the linen cloths but rolled up in a place by itself. [8]Then the other disciple who had reached the tomb first also went in; he saw and he believed. [9]Till this moment they had failed to understand the teaching of scripture, that he must rise from the dead. [10]The disciples then went home again.

The appearance to Mary of Magdala

[11]Meanwhile Mary stayed outside near the tomb, weeping. Then, still weeping, she stooped to look inside, [12]and saw two angels in white sitting where the body of Jesus had been, one at the head, the other at the feet. [13]They said, 'Woman, why are you weeping?' 'They have taken my Lord away' she replied 'and I don't know where they have put him.' [14]As she said this she turned round and saw Jesus standing there, though she did not recognise him. [15]Jesus said, 'Woman, why are you weeping? Who are you looking for?' Supposing him to be the gardener, she said, 'Sir, if you have taken him away, tell me where you have put him, and I will go and remove him'. [16]Jesus said, 'Mary!' She knew him then and said to him in Hebrew, 'Rabbuni!' - which means Master. [17]Jesus said to her, 'Do not cling to me, because I have not yet ascended to the Father. But go and find the brothers, and tell them: I am ascending to my Father and your Father, to my God

and your God.' [18]So Mary of Magdala went and told the disciples that she had seen the Lord and that he had said these things to her.

Appearances to the disciples

[19]In the evening of that same day, the first day of the week, the doors were closed in the room where the disciples were, for fear of the Jews. Jesus came and stood among them. He said to them, 'Peace be with you', [20]and showed them his hands and his side. The disciples were filled with joy when they saw the Lord, [21]and he said to them again, 'Peace be with you.

'As the Father sent me,

so am I sending you.'

[22]After saying this he breathed on them and said:

'Receive the Holy Spirit.

[23]For those whose sins you forgive,

they are forgiven;

for those whose sins you retain,

they are retained.'

[24]Thomas, called the Twin, who was one of the Twelve, was not with them when Jesus came. [25]When the disciples said, 'We have seen the Lord', he answered, 'Unless I see the holes that the nails made in his hands and can put my finger into the holes they made, and unless I can put my hand into his side, I refuse to believe'. [26]Eight days later the disciples were in the house again and Thomas was with them. The doors were closed, but Jesus came in and stood among them. 'Peace be

with you' he said. [27]Then he spoke to Thomas, 'Put your finger here; look, here are my hands. Give me your hand; put it into my side. Doubt no longer but believe.' [28]Thomas replied, 'My Lord and my God!' [29]Jesus said to him:

'You believe because you can see me.

Happy are those who have not seen and yet believe.'

CONCLUSION

[30]There were many other signs that Jesus worked and the disciples saw, but they are not recorded in this book. [31]These are recorded so that you may believe that Jesus is the Christ, the Son of God, and that believing this you may have life through his name.

APPENDIX[a]

The appearance on the shore of Tiberias

21 [1]Later on, Jesus showed himself again to the disciples. It was by the Sea of Tiberias, and it happened like this: [2]Simon Peter, Thomas called the Twin, Nathanael from Cana in Galilee, the sons of Zebedee and two more of his disciples were together. [3]Simon Peter said, 'I'm going fishing'. They replied, 'We'll come with you'. They went out and got into the boat but caught nothing that night.

[4]It was light by now and there stood Jesus on the shore, though the disciples did not realise that it was Jesus. [5]Jesus called out, 'Have you caught anything, friends?'

[21 a.] Added either by the evangelist or by a disciple of his.

And when they answered, 'No', ⁶he said, 'Throw the net out to starboard and you'll find something'. So they dropped the net, and there were so many fish that they could not haul it in. ⁷The disciple Jesus loved said to Peter, 'It is the Lord'. At these words 'It is the Lord', Simon Peter, who had practically nothing on, wrapped his cloak round him and jumped into the water. ⁸The other disciples came on in the boat, towing the net and the fish; they were only about a hundred yards from land.

⁹As soon as they came ashore they saw that there was some bread there, and a charcoal fire with fish cooking on it. ¹⁰Jesus said, 'Bring some of the fish you have just caught'. ¹¹Simon Peter went aboard and dragged the net to the shore, full of big fish, one hundred and fifty-three of them; and in spite of there being so many the net was not broken. ¹²Jesus said to them, 'Come and have breakfast'. None of the disciples was bold enough to ask, 'Who are you?'; they knew quite well it was the Lord. ¹³Jesus then stepped forward, took the bread and gave it to them, and the same with the fish. ¹⁴This was the third time that Jesus showed himself to the disciples after rising from the dead.

¹⁵After the meal Jesus said to Simon Peter, 'Simon son of John, do you love me more than these others do?' He answered, 'Yes Lord, you know I love you'. Jesus said to him, 'Feed my lambs'. ¹⁶A second time he said to him, 'Simon son of John, do you love me?' He replied, 'Yes,

Lord, you know I love you'. Jesus said to him, 'Look after my sheep'. [17]Then he said to him a third time, 'Simon son of John, do you love me?' Peter was upset that he asked him the third time, 'Do you love me?' and said, 'Lord, you know everything; you know I love you'. Jesus said to him, 'Feed my sheep.

[18]'I tell you most solemnly,
when you were young
you put on your own belt
and walked where you liked;
but when you grow old
you will stretch out your hands,
and somebody else will put a belt round you
and take you where you would rather not go.'

[19]In these words he indicated the kind of death by which Peter would give glory to God. After this he said, 'Follow me'.

[20]Peter turned and saw the disciple Jesus loved following them - the one who had leaned on his breast at the supper and had said to him, 'Lord, who is it that will betray you?' [21]Seeing him, Peter said to Jesus, 'What about him, Lord?' [22]Jesus answered, 'If I want him to stay behind till I come, what does it matter to you? You are to follow me.' [23]The rumour then went out among the brothers that this disciple would not die. Yet Jesus had not said to Peter, 'He will not die', but, 'If I want him to stay behind till I come'.

Conclusion

[24]This disciple is the one who vouches for these things and has written them down, and we know that his testimony is true.

[25]There were many other things that Jesus did; if all were written down, the world itself, I suppose, would not hold all the books that would have to be written.